IF YOUR CHILD IS GAY

WHAT EVERY PARENT OF A GAY CHILD NEEDS TO KNOW TO
INSURE A POSITIVE OUTCOME IN AN OFTEN NEGATIVE WORLD

2nd Edition

by

REV. STEVE KINDLE

EnerPower Press
Gonzalez, FL
2016

ISBN10: 1-63199-224-4
ISBN13: 978-1-63199-224-7
Library of Congress Control Number: 2016935517

EnerPower Press
P. O. Box 841
Gonzalez, FL 32560

energion.com
pubs@energion.com
(EnerPower Press is an imprint of Energion Publications)

Dedication

To Mary Lou Wallner,
and all parents who struggle to find answers

Contents

FOREWORD

This book is intended to introduce parents of gay children to the many findings from the professional psychologists, sociologists and theologians who have given their lives to understand your gay child. It will also be reassuring to adolescent LGBTs and older. It will introduce you to many parents who have gone before you in their quest for understanding and who want to share their wisdom with you. It is packed with helpful advice and places to go for help. It's a way to begin and a launching pad for further discovery. Should you wish to delve deeper into specific areas, you will be shown where to go.

I am a straight pastor who began my ministry over 40 years ago with the conventional beliefs of the day that saw homosexuality as a psychological deviance and a religious sin. I believed that LGBTs chose this lifestyle and could change if they wanted to. Of course, I was not familiar with the many studies you will be introduced to in this book, or much more importantly, I was not familiar with gays themselves. Over the years, I have gotten to know many hundreds of LGBTs, even into the thousands, heard their stories, helped them work through their fears, and find their way in an often hostile world. Being instrumental in reconciling parents with their gay children is one of my proudest accomplishments and the genesis for this book. I want you and your family to be among the success stories.

Many who read these pages will come with religious convictions, one way or another. The scientific professionals are not the only ones who have been involved in how to understand homosexuality. Biblical scholars have for decades been delving into the Bible, examining everything that relates to these issues. What they have discovered is also a part of this book. The combined efforts of the scientists and biblical scholars can be summed up in the words of Dr. Mel White. "The verdict is in; it is not a sickness, it is not a sin." So, let's begin.

INTRODUCTION

The "coming out" process for any LGBT person, especially to one's family, is often a very traumatic experience. What is often overlooked is the trauma visited upon the family, especially on the unsuspecting and now overwhelmed parents.

Mom and dad are very often confronted with a whole new world that they previously knew little or nothing about. Although suspicions of same-sex orientation may have lurked in the background, they are often quickly dismissed; the possibility is too dire to entertain. At least that's what is often thought.

There are many voices of concern out there urging many different approaches. So, where does a parent begin? To whom or what can a parent turn for help? How can the proper information be separated from the harmful or just plain ignorant? These and other questions will be answered as we move from section to section. I write from the perspective of a straight pastor of over 40 years who has been confronted with just about every situation a parent can experience, including counseling dozens of parents and hundreds of gay children. You may feel that no one else has gone through what you are experiencing right now, but you will soon discover there is much company for you with people who have gone on before.

This book is intended to assist parents who are genuinely trying to understand their gay children. If you are such a parent, the sooner you get involved with your child with understanding and support, the better the outcome will be for all concerned. You don't have to have all the answers, or any for that matter. All you need to begin is to acknowledge that your child is no different today from the one you brought into the world, that your love is the same and continues, and that nothing can change that. If you truly believe this, the rest of these sections will help you. If you can't affirm your love for your child, get counseling immediately; studies show that suicides are a greater risk following parental rejection. I don't tell you this to make you feel worse, it is a fact that you need to know and consider.

Over the next several sections, these are the subjects we will look into. We will take them one at a time.

You are not alone

What is the LGBT(QIA) thing?

Your child is just fine

You are not to blame

Will my son get HIV/AIDS?

What if my child is Transgender? Navigating the intersexual world

The Bible doesn't condemn your child

Marriage is a good possibility

You still may have grandchildren

The Anti-gay Industry

Great resource for more help and understanding

At the end of almost every section you will find a link to a video or article that will offer further explanations and insights from authorities in the field or people going through similar experiences as yours. Just copy the link and transfer it to your online device.

If you take advantage of the support available to you now, you may never have to face the worst fate for a parent, as explained by Mary Lou Wallner (to whom this book is dedicated) in this 5 minute video.

http://youtu.be/ycbHnPhw8VQ

You Are Not Alone

That's right, you are not alone. It may not feel that way at first; you may feel there is no one to talk to, no one to turn to for help, no one you can trust with what you just heard. Perhaps not even your spouse. Yet your mind is racing with questions: Will my child be alright? Will she be safe? Will he lose his job, or friends, or church? Is she going to hell? What can I do? Can she change? Is it my fault? Will I never have the joy of grandchildren?

Know that for these questions to surface, and more, is normal. After all, you are likely entering into a world you are not familiar with, so it feels uncharted, and you are set adrift, but you are not alone.

The very first thing I would encourage you to do is to talk to a knowledgeable person. Get in touch with others who have faced the same situation. Mothers and fathers of gay children are all around you, but because you have not needed to know this, they aren't on your landscape. See if there is a PFLAG (Parents and Friends of Lesbians and Gays) chapter near you. If there is, you will immediately learn that you and your child are in good company where you will meet others who have gone through the same experience and found hope.

If you are reluctant to go to a public meeting, most PFLAG folk would be happy to meet you and discuss personal issues with you and/or your child. What is most important now is for you to connect with others who can support you positively through this time.

If a PFLAG chapter is not an option, contact a clergy person from the United Church of Christ, the Unitarian Universalist Church, the Christian Church (Disciples of Christ) or any church in the Yellow Pages or online in your community that advertises itself as either "Open and Affirming," or the Methodist's "Reconciling Congregation," or the Presbyterian's "More Light congregation." Lacking these, call an Episcopal priest or anyone in the local Interfaith community. Ask them to recommend a gay-friendly person to talk to. If you are fortunate to have a church nearby that supports gay inclusion, you will get good answers to your most urgent and vexing questions.

Your child will have many questions as well. The PFLAG website has several documents that you can download that are very helpful for both parent and child. Here's the link to their highly rated and most requested resource for parents, http://community.pflag.org/document.doc?id=495, "Our Sons and Daughters: Questions and Answers for Parents of Gay, Lesbian and Bisexual People." Here's the link for your child: http://www.pflag.org/fileadmin/user_upload/Publications/Be_Yourself.pdf. "Be Yourself: Questions and Answers for Gay, Lesbian, Bisexual and Transgender Youth."

If all else fails, contact me at info@clergyunited.org, and I will personally assist you and keep everything in confidence.

There is currently running an ad campaign that tells gay youth, "It gets better!" This is just as true for parents of gay children. It gets better! The sooner you contact a supporting person or group, the better you will feel, not only about your child, but about yourself, as someone who can continue to be the loving, supporting parent you have been and will continue to be.

http://youtu.be/2DWzmYO0D8Y

WHAT IS THIS
LGBT(QI) THING?

I f you are new to the world of the gay community, you will soon be introduced to a variety of terms and acronyms that are in general use, most of which are self-explanatory, but not all. The most frequently used and often stands for the entire gay community is LGBT: An acronym for lesbian, gay, bisexual, and transgender which refers to these individuals collectively. It is sometimes stated as GLBT (gay, lesbian, bi, and transgender). Occasionally, the acronym is stated as LGBTA to include allies – straight and supportive individuals. The acronym sometimes includes Q for queer or questioning. (All definitions come from the PFLAG website and documents and OutFront Minnesota.)

Lesbian: A woman whose enduring emotional, romantic, physical, and/or spiritual attraction is to other women. Avoid identifying lesbians as homosexuals, which is often seen as a derogatory term.

Gay: The adjective used to describe people whose enduring emotional, romantic, physical, and/or spiritual attractions are to people of the same sex (e.g., gay man, gay people). In contemporary contexts, lesbian is often a preferred term for women.

Bisexual: An individual who is emotionally, romantically, physically, and/or spiritually attracted to men and women. Bisexuals do not need to have had equal sexual experience with both men and women; in fact, they need not have had any sexual experience at all to identify as bisexual. Sometimes stated as bi.

Transgender: A term describing the state of a person's gender identity which does not necessarily match his/her assigned sex at birth. Other words commonly used are female to male (FTM), male to female (MTF), and genderqueer. Transgender people may or may not decide to alter their bodies hormonally and/or surgically to match their gender identity.

Queer: Traditionally a negative or pejorative term for gay, queer currently is used by some LGBTs—particularly among younger people —to describe themselves and/or their community. Some value the term for its defiance, some like it because it can be inclusive of the entire community, and others find it to be an appropriate term to describe their more fluid identities. Many within the LGBT community continue to dislike the term and find it offensive. This word should be avoided by straights (non LGBTpeople).

Intersexual: Having both male and female anatomical characteristics, including in varying degrees reproductive organs and secondary sexual characteristics, as a result of an abnormality of the sex chromosomes or a hormonal imbalance during embryogenesis. (This definition is from the Free Online Dictionary) These were once known as hermaphrodite.

Ally: Any non-LGBTQI who supports gay rights and equality.

If you don't recognize your child here, you might ask him or her to give you their take on the ins and outs of this acronym as a way for each of you to understand yourselves better. There are quite a few more terms and acronyms that you will encounter, but this list is the most used and will get you going.

What's most important to know is that LGBTIQs will be very patient with you if they sense that your intentions are to relate, not to judge. Any crossing of that line will be noted immediately and may harm what could be fruitful dialog and hopefully a lifelong and healthy relationship.

One other thing: The gay community is not monolithic. There is some disagreement as to the usefulness and meanings of this acronym. So it's best not to assume you share the same frame of reference. Be a good listener.

Here's some great advice from a young lady:
http://youtu.be/CMSBc2hOQK0

YOUR CHILD IS JUST FINE

You need assurance that your child is all right, not because there is any doubt in the minds of professionals, but because of society's fear of the different, the "other," that has made even left-handedness suspicious. So false stereotypes exist that continue to make life uneasy for you and your child. You may also worry because bullying and overt discrimination work against those who are perceived as different. I don't want to lead you to believe that life will be rosy. On the contrary, there will be obstacles in the way of your child that are not present for straight children. But there is a lot of good will and support available to you, as well.

I am concerned, first of all, that you understand that there is nothing psychologically, physiologically, or mentally about your child that is considered unusual or cause for concern.

Listen carefully to these representative professionals:

The American Psychological Association released a Statement on Homosexuality in July of 1994. The opening paragraphs are:

> The research on homosexuality is very clear. Homosexuality is neither mental illness nor moral depravity. It is simply the way a minority of our population expresses

human love and sexuality. Study after study documents
the mental health of gay men and lesbians. Studies of
judgment, stability, reliability, and social and vocational
adaptiveness all show that gay men and lesbians function
every bit as well as heterosexuals.

Nor is homosexuality a matter of individual choice.
Research suggests that the homosexual orientation is
in place very early in the life cycle, possibly even before
birth. It is found in about ten percent of the population,
a figure which is surprisingly constant across cultures,
irrespective of the different moral values and standards
of a particular culture. Contrary to what some imply,
the incidence of homosexuality in a population does not
appear to change with new moral codes or social mores.
Research findings suggest that efforts to repair homosexuals are nothing more than social prejudice garbed in
psychological accouterments.

This affirmation of the normalcy of gays and lesbians runs
across the board of professional associations, including the American Psychiatric Association, the American Academy of Pediatrics,
the American Medical Association, American Counseling Association, American Association of School Administrators, American
Federation of Teachers, American School Health Association,
Interfaith Alliance Foundation, National Association of School
Psychologists, National Association of Social Workers, and the National Education Association. Therefore, if you have any fear that
your child may be somehow deficient as a human being, put those
fears away for good. There is no basis for it except in the minds of
those who refuse to look at these overwhelming facts.

The biggest obstacle to understanding the normalcy of nonheterosexuals is not knowing many or any. As long as we insulate
ourselves from the community, we will never get to see them as they
actually are. When I first moved to San Francisco, I took with me
all the negative stereotypes that had formed me as a young man.

Yes, the flamboyancy was there, the sexual promiscuity was there. But what I soon discovered was the promiscuity of my straight peers was its equal, and that the gay community as a whole was no different from any other. They were also forming families, raising children, going to church, and leading very indistinguishable lives. In fact, being gay is so ordinary that most gays are not identifiable without self-labeling. You are living among many of them and you don't even know it. This may possibly even include your own child.

If you take the step to inform yourself by going to gay community centers or PFLAG meetings, for instance, you will see what I mean. If there is an Open and Affirming church in your community, that's a great place to begin. Once, African Americans were considered inferior, and were not allowed to marry whites in some states (up to 1964!). Now one is the president of the United States. We were able to see this remarkable transition unfold in a lifetime because whites got to know blacks and the stereotypes were debunked. The more we get to know our gay and lesbian neighbors, the quicker we will move as a society away from their crude and highly misleading stereotypes.

So, your child is normal. Well, kind of, and in an OK kind of way: http://www.youtube.com/watch?feature=player_embedded&v=vjXUjH5IdCI

WILL MY SON GET HIV/AIDS?

want to begin this section by exploding one of the most pernicious myths circulating about the gay community, and particularly about gay men. Here is what purports to be the results of a scientific study led by a supposedly reputable researcher. Dr. Paul Cameron.

How long did homosexuals live before the AIDS epidemic and how long do they live today? We examined 6,737 obituaries/death notices from eighteen U.S. homosexual journals over the past thirteen years and compared them to obituaries from two conventional newspapers. The obituaries from the non-homosexual newspapers were similar to U.S. averages for longevity: the median age of death of married men was seventy-five, 80 percent died old (65 or older); for unmarried men it was fifty-seven, 32 percent died old; for married women it was seventy-nine, 85 percent died old; for unmarried women it was seventy-one, 60 percent died old. For the 6,574 homosexual deaths, the median age of death if AIDS was the cause was thirty-nine irrespective of whether or not the individual had a Long Time Sexual Partner [LTSP], 1 percent died old. For those 829 who died of non-AIDS

causes the median age of death was forty-two (41 for
those 315 with a LTSP and 43 for those 514 without)
and < 9 percent died old. Homosexuals more frequently
met a violent end from accidental death, traffic death,
suicide, and murder than men in general. The 163 lesbians registered a median age of death of forty-four (20%
died old) and exhibited high rates of violent death and
cancer as compared to women in general. Old homosexuals appear to have been proportionately less numerous
than their non-homosexual counterparts in the scientific
literature from 1858 to 1993. The pattern of early death
evident in the homosexual obituaries is consistent with
the pattern exhibited in the published surveys of homosexuals and intravenous drug abusers. Homosexuals may
have experienced a short lifespan for the last 140 years;
AIDS has apparently reduced it about 10 percent. Such
an abbreviated lifespan puts the healthfulness of homosexuality in question.

This summation of Cameron's "research" was pulled from his
organization's website after receiving incredible denunciation from
peer reviewed journals. He now offers an equally nonsensical explanation at www.familyresearchinst.com. Due to this and other
spurious "results," Cameron has been removed from memberships
in the Nebraska Psychological Association, and The American Psychological Association. In a court case, Baker Vs. Wade, a District
Court Judge called Cameron's sworn statement, "fraud."

If this study were to be believed, parents of gay children would
have much to fear for their child. But it is not to be believed.
Neither are the notions that gay men are more promiscuous than
straight men. In fact, a study of the sexual habits of four million
gay men recently published in the UK establishes that

There is only a one percentage point difference
between heterosexuals and homosexuals in their promiscuity: 98% of gay people have had 20 or fewer sexual

partners; 99% of straight people have had the same
number. Tellingly, OkCupid found that it is just 2% of
gay people that are having 23% of the total reported gay
sex. (http://www.guardian.co.uk/commentisfree/2010/
oct/19/gay-men-promiscuous-myth)

HIV/AIDS is a relevant issue for gays and straights. Young
gay men are being infected at a larger rate than others because they
are growing up in an era where AIDS is not the killer it once was.
So they think, as most young people do, that they are immune to
it and will live forever. Unprotected sex is the culprit.

However, just because a person reveals ("comes out") that he
or she is gay, does not necessarily mean that sexual activity is involved. It could be nothing more than attraction at work with no
acting out.

On the other hand, the chances are good that sexual activity is
present or soon will be. This is where good parenting comes into
play and why it is good that you now know. There are many sources
of information available to parents and youth that make for good
discussion opportunities than can lead to greater understanding.
http://www.wikihow.com/Avoid-Getting-AIDS and http://www.
livestrong.com/article/80154-avoid-aids/ will get you started. The
sooner you have this talk, the better, for knowing this information
is the first step toward staying HIV free.

I know many Christian sources advocate sexual abstinence
until marriage as the only protection against HIV/AIDS, but studies show that this is one of the least effective means. Although the
question singles out gay males, it is a much broader issue that affects
both men and women, gay and straight, and people of all ages.

Here's a primer on AIDS: http://youtu.be/4taixWFjWWI

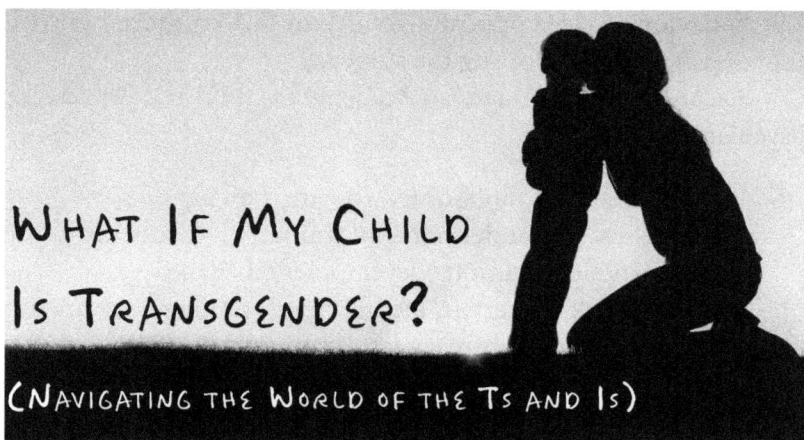

WHAT IF MY CHILD IS TRANSGENDER?
(NAVIGATING THE WORLD OF THE Ts AND Is)

The T and I in LGBTI are likely the most foreign and off-putting sexualities in the acronym for those not familiar with the people they represent. One of the cruelest tricks nature can play on someone is to realize that your body says you are of one gender, but your heart and mind tell you that you are really of another gender. So you may appear to be, say, a boy, but inside you know you are a girl (or just the opposite). In the extreme case, you are born with what is termed "ambiguous genitalia," that is, having both male and female sexual organs to some extent. The normal course of action, until recently, was "gender assignment" at birth, where the parents decided what gender the child would be brought up as, and the offending genitalia were surgically removed. This often created conflicted feelings in the child that caused permanent harm. The trend now is for the child to remain "ambiguous" until he or she can name one's own sexuality. These, termed intersexuals, are now considered a normal, if relatively rare form of human sexuality. It is estimated that one to two births in 100 are intersex.

Those with normal genitalia, yet totally rejecting that gender role, often opt for "gender reassignment" surgery, which is preceded by hormone therapy and rigorous psychological study, and live comfortably as the other sex from then on. These are the T or transgender. (Note: not transgendered.) Others adopt the dress and behavior of their opposite gender to feel comfortable with themselves, without electing the surgery.

According to the American Academy of Child and Adolescent Psychiatry:

> Children and adolescents who are growing up gay, lesbian, bisexual, gender nonconforming, or gender discordant experience unique developmental challenges.
> They are at risk for certain mental health problems, many of which are significantly correlated with stigma and prejudice.

If we lived in a world where LGBTI children were allowed to grow up without societal prejudice, most of the problems now associated with their lives would never materialize. But we don't have such a society. So the parents of these children need to provide as much safety and nurture as they can. This will have to involve professionals trained in these areas, as most of us are not equipped to cover all the issues. So my advice is to surround yourself with as many people and services as possible who are informed and truly want to aid you in your journey.

Now for a side issue. Some Christians associate T and I with the Mosaic denunciation that, *A woman shall not wear a man's apparel, nor shall a man put on a woman's garment; for whoever does such things is abhorrent to the Lord your God* (Deuteronomy 22:5).

This is interpreted to mean that Moses denounces any kind of altering of sexual patterns. As for this being "abhorrent," see the section on Leviticus, coming up. Two things need to be kept in mind. First, the Mosaic Law was concerned with conformity. The natural was considered to be a certain (arbitrary) form. For example, a fish has scales, so catfish are unclean and an abomination. Scales as a deciding factor is arbitrary, as we now know fish are many things. So men need to conform to what a man is and women to what a woman is. Second, sociologists suggest that in harem societies, this law was intended to keep men from sneaking into a harem and violating the harem owner's rights.

If your child is struggling with gender identification issues, you have an opportunity to make a significant and highly valuable contribution to his or her well-being. The worst course is to take a combative approach, for it will mean heartache for you and emotional issues for your child. Get the best help you can now.

Here's a comprehensive article that looks at how parents can understand and help their transgender child lead as normal a life as possible: http://www.trans-parenting.com/understanding-gender/faq/.

IT'S NOT YOUR FAULT (IT'S GOD'S!)

When things don't go well for their children, parents often blame themselves for negative outcomes. They wonder what they might have done differently. Add to this the many false theories on what causes homosexuality, and you have a perfect set up for a parental guilt trip.

One of the most egregious pseudoscientific theories tries to convince parents that distant fathers and overbearing mothers produce gay children. Consequently, many parents feel responsible for their children not being "normal."

A few years ago I attended a lecture by the chief proponent of this theory, known as Reparative Therapy (or Conversion Therapy), Dr. Joseph Nicolosi.

After it was over, I asked him why I turned out to be straight when my parents fit his model perfectly. "Well," he said, "It doesn't always work that way." It sure doesn't, and for good reason. Every respectable professional association not only condemns this theory, but also labels it positively harmful. It promotes needless guilt in parents and holds out false hope that gays can be "returned" to heterosexuality.

Here's a summary statement taken from ReligiousTollerance.org:

The American Psychiatric Association removed
homosexuality from its list of mental illnesses in 1973.
The American Psychological Association followed suit
in 1975; the National Association of Social Workers in
1977; the National Psychoanalytic Association finally followed suit in 1991, stating that homosexuality was not a
disorder. The American Academy of Pediatrics, American
Counseling Association, American Association of School
Administrators, American Federation of Teachers, American Psychological Association, American School Health
Association, Interfaith Alliance Foundation, National
Association of School Psychologists, National Association
of Social Workers, and National Education Association
formed the "Just the Facts Coalition." They developed
and endorsed "Just the Facts About Sexual Orientation
& Youth: A Primer for Principals, Educators and School
Personnel" in 1999.

The primer says, in part:

"The most important fact about 'reparative therapy,'
also sometimes known as 'conversion' therapy, is that
it is based on an understanding of homosexuality that
has been rejected by all the major health and mental
health professions. The American Academy of Pediatrics,
the American Counseling Association, the American
Psychiatric Association, the American Psychological Association, the National Association of School Psychologists,
and the National Association of Social Workers, together representing more than 477,000 health and mental
health professionals, have all taken the position that homosexuality is not a mental disorder and thus there is no
need for a 'cure.'

In January 2012, Exodus International president Alan Chambers unexpectedly came out against the view that gays can be made

straight. Here's the full quote: "The majority of [gay] people that I have met, and I would say the majority meaning 99.9% of them, have not experienced a change in their orientation." (Full article here: http://www.boxturtlebulletin.com/2012/01/09/40435) Interestingly, that would likely include Chambers himself, who has for years claimed an orientation change. Exodus International was the leading organization contending that gays can change and is now defunct.

I have in my files on a CD, a speech from a former member of EI's board of directors suggesting that, since a preponderance of gays don't change, Exodus International should change its motto from "Change is possible through Jesus Christ," to "Come suffer with us."

There has been only one "scientific" study that has held that gays do change. It was conducted by none other than the psychologist who led the American Psychological Association to remove homosexuality from the list of mental disorders in 1973, Dr. Robert Spitzer. It was his presumed objectivity that gave the study its prestige. Recently, Dr. Spitzer retracted his study with an apology to the gay community for the harm he had caused. Here is the text of the written apology:

> I believe I owe the gay community an apology for my study making unproven claims of the efficacy of reparative therapy. I also apologize to any gay person who wasted time and energy undergoing some form of reparative therapy because they believed that I had proven that reparative therapy works with some 'highly motivated' individuals. Robert Spitzer. M.D.

The most important thing I believe parents of gay children should take from these professionals is that there is absolutely nothing to be concerned about. No one did anything wrong, and your kids are perfectly normal. This is not to say that there will be no issues associated with gayness that you and your child will have to face. However, these conditions are a product of society's ill-formed picture of what being gay is all about. Fortunately, they are diminishing at a rapid rate, so quickly in fact that now a majority of Americans support the recent Supreme Court of the United States decision to legalize same-sex marriage.

Charles Darwin's conviction that the origin of sexual orientation is one of humanity's deepest secrets, available to no one, is still true. One thing is for certain, parent—you are not the reason you have a gay child. If there is a God, and I believe there is, God made us all the way we are.

Here's a video with a Ph.D. discussing "reparative therapy."
http://www.youtube.com/watch?feature=player_embedded&v=Kh6v9aysfQI

Marriage Is Still
A Good Possibility

W hat is it that virtually all parents want for their children? That's easy: we want them to be happy.

Let's go on a little side trip. One of the most destructive aspects of LGBTs living in the closet is that many of them will try to cover up their sexual orientation by getting married. In many cases, this is done with affection, but not with love. That is, it does not satisfy their deepest longing. And it is not only to conceal a secret, but, often, to make parents happy. Almost every mom and dad yearns for grandchildren. So, believing that revealing their sexual orientation will crush their parent's dreams, they give opposite sex marriage a go. These are known as "mixed-orientation marriages."

The results are devastating to all parties involved.

According to Amity Buxton of the Straight Spouse Network,

> When the gay, lesbian, or bisexual spouse comes out, a third of the couples break up immediately; another third stay together for one to two years, sorting out what to do and then divorce; the remaining third try to make their marriages work. Half of these couples divorce, while half of them (17% of the total) stay together for three or more years.

The Family Pride Coalition compiled the following statistics:

» 20 percent of all gay men in America are in a heterosexual marriage.

» 50 percent of all gay men in America have fathered children.

» 40 percent of all lesbians in America are married to a male partner.

» 75 percent of all lesbians have children." (From a story on About.com by Sheri & Bob Stritof, About.com Guides)

Almost every LGBT I know over 40 tried, unsuccessfully, the marriage route. Most had children. But because the effort "to live a lie" (their words) was more than they could bear, divorce eventually followed. Imagine the poor spouses left alone, the children, now bewildered, and most importantly, what could have been. All this because society had no way of understanding the legitimacy of their orientation and could not make the necessary adjustment to allow for the one thing that would make them happy: same-sex marriage.

So, if as a parent you want your child to be happy, you should foster an environment where they will be free to follow their own dreams for themselves, and not live out your own.

Fortunately, the tide is turning and now a majority of Americans are for giving LGBTs the freedom to marry. This, along with the United States Supreme Court's decision to make marriage equality legal across the nation, is creating an environment that makes it possible for LGBTs to consider same-sex marriage for themselves when before it was only a vague hope.

Now that it is possible for LGBTs to marry one of their own orientation, it will end many injustices simultaneously: divorce, children of divorce, unsatisfactory life arrangements, and make possible the one thing parents want most for their children, their happiness.

The following video shows both the devastation and the hope that are both found when LGBTs marry other than of their natural orientation. Watch it, and weep for all those who continue to struggle.

http://www.youtube.com/watch?feature=player_embedded&v=xkKoD1uVbrE

YOU STILL MAY HAVE GRANDCHILDREN

According to the US Census Bureau's data from 2010, the number of children in LGBT households doubled since 2000. And 25% of the children are biologically related to one of the parents. Adoption accounts for the rest. The trend continues into this decade as states are making it easier for gay couples to adopt.

According to the American Fertility Association, Arkansas, California, Colorado, Connecticut, Illinois, Massachusetts, New Jersey, New York, Pennsylvania, Vermont, and the District of Columbia allow gay or lesbian stepparents to adopt their partners' children. Except for Pennsylvania, those states also allow any other same-sex couples to adopt, as do Indiana, Iowa, Maine, Nevada, New Hampshire, Oregon, Vermont, and Washington. North Dakota, Oklahoma, Louisiana, Mississippi, Ohio, and New Hampshire specifically prohibit it. All states except Florida allow a single LGBT person to adopt.

This trend toward expanding the right of gay couples to adopt is driven, in part, by research which shows that children are not adversely affected by being raised by same-sex couples. The American Psychological Association states in their official policy that "research has shown that the adjustment, development, and psychological well-being of children is unrelated to parental sexual orientation and that the children of lesbian and gay parents are as likely as those of heterosexual parents to flourish." http://www.apa.org/about/policy/parenting.aspx There is also no qualitative difference between the love of same-sex couples for their children and that of heterosexual couples. To those who think otherwise, I have only one response: you don't know enough LGBTs who have formed families and been together for decades.

Same-sex couples are forming families at an astonishing rate with the increased acceptance of gay normalcy across America. So, if you are the parent of an LGBT child, your chances of becoming a grandparent are still very good. This is just another of the many ways that, once people get to know LGBTs and their families, they turn out to be little different from any other families we know.

One of the arguments against same-sex marriage is that gays can't procreate. But marriage is for many more things than pro-creation. With all the orphans that need good homes, it seems to me that LGBT families offer a great service to the rest of us when they take one or more into their homes.

Hear from gay parents who have adopted in this video:
http://www.youtube.com/watch?feature=player_embedded&v=2-cB0tDBgpM

WHAT DOES THE BIBLE SAY?

This section is by far the longest because biblical textual abuse is one of the greatest obstacles in overcoming our deep-seated, yet largely unexamined sources for assuming that the Bible condemns homosexuality. If you are a Christian, or at least understand that you may have been influenced by those who use the Bible against gays, please read on. If you are not a Christian and don't care what the Bible says, you are excused to move on to the next section. However, many of your family and friends continue to be influenced by outmoded biblical interpretations and you might want to know this information in discussing the issues with them.

The ultimate recourse for those who want to keep homosexuality on the sins list is, "My Bible says...." The sentence generally ends with "...homosexuals are an abomination," or, "...gays are going to hell," or "…God hates gays." This is intended to be the final word on the matter; the Bible has spoken, the issue is clear, we can move on to other things. How so? Because the Bible has spoken.

The Bible, of course says no such thing. The Bible "says" nothing. It is an inert object, words on paper. It can't utter a sound. What is really going on is that people say the Bible says something; people speak on behalf of the Bible. The Bible is deaf and mute.

Unfortunately, people too often make what "the Bible says" what they want it to say. You see, there is no such thing as an uninterpreted reading of anything, from the daily newspaper to the Bible. All of us read (or "hear what it says") though a filter or a lens. No one can read without one. Your filter/lens is everything that you have learned through your culture, ethnicity, gender, nationality, education...you get the point...that shapes how you perceive meaning. Every word you read or hear is processed through this filtering system. Everyone reads or hears the same word or words differently. Depending on how far apart our systems are, we can basically understand each other or totally misunderstand. In explaining this to an adult Sunday School class, one member said, "I can think of something we both read that needs no filtering, that is straightforward and immediately understood." "Okay," I said. "Let's have it." He responded, "God is love." I replied with, "What do you mean by 'God' and what do you mean by 'love'"? He got my point.

When it comes to reading the Bible, we have a two to three thousand year old bridge to cross. We need to be able to "hear" as though we were an immediate member of the culture of those who created those biblical words. This is virtually impossible. The best we can do is approximate this; we will never actually achieve this. And even for those who were contemporaries, they had their own problems. Here's Peter's comment on Paul's letters: *There are some things in them hard to understand.* (2 Peter 2:16) Indeed.

So the next time you are tempted to tell someone what the Bible says, why not be honest and tell them that you think this is what the Bible, properly interpreted, means. You will have achieved two things. First, you will have admitted that your interpretation is open to opinion (and that it is your opinion), and that you might be, dare I say it...wrong.

We will now take a look at the few passages that have been interpreted as antigay.

Why God approves of Adam and Steve as well as Adam and Eve

Maggie Gallagher quotes Norval Glenn in her book, *The Case for Marriage*:

> Most social scientists who have studied the data believe that marriage itself accounts for a great deal of the difference in average well-being between married and unmarried persons. Indeed, loneliness is probably the negative feeling most likely to be alleviated simply by being married. (p.77)

Gallagher and Glenn are on to something here. Loneliness is a universal condition which the Bible addresses from the very beginning. Human loneliness is at the heart of the marriage issue, although not well understood or articulated by either side. Ending human loneliness is crucial, not simply because it is an onerous human condition that no one unwillingly should be made to bear, but because it is the fundamental human predicament that first surfaced in the Genesis story of creation that caused God to reevaluate the human being.

From Genesis, Chapter 2, it is clear that God's first intention for the human being, *ha 'adam* was not heterosexuality or even sexuality, for *ha 'adam* was created as a "stand alone" being. In other words, no other creature was intended. Don't be confused by Chapter 1 where in verse 27 we read, *So God created humankind in his image, in the image of God he created them; male and female he created them.* This is, of course, true (and obviates the overt patriarchalism of the story). However, it is a summary statement that concludes the events of Chapter 2, a much earlier story of creation than Chapter 1. So we need to read Chapter 2 before the summary of Chapter 1 can make sense.

The story begins with God creating *ha 'adam* as someone who would be placed in charge of the garden, to care for and tend it with God as partner. For reasons not disclosed, God observes that it is not good for *ha 'adam* to be alone, and goes about making a suitable helper for him.

What happens next is unexpected and likely a surprise to some: the first thing God does to provide a suitable helper for the man is NOT to create a woman but to create animals and bring them to the man for his approval. Chapter 2:20 says, *The man gave names to all cattle, and to the birds of the air, and to every animal of the field; but for the man there was not found a helper as his partner.* We must take this seriously as an authentic effort on God's behalf to find for *ha 'adam* a suitable partner.

The first thing that strikes me about Genesis is that the picture of God's nature is very different from what I, as a young Sunday School student, was taught to believe. That God can be said to be omnipotent, omniscient, and omnipresent may be true, but having said that, one does not necessarily understand how it works out in reality. One of the longstanding arguments in theology relates to this: Does God know everything that will happen before it happens? (As with the Calvinists.) Or, does God limit God's omniscience to allow unhampered free will? (As with the Arminians.)

Interestingly, Genesis sides with the latter. On at least three occasions in the Torah God is found NOT to know the consequences of God's actions.

The first is found in Genesis 6:5-7:

> *The LORD saw that the wickedness of humankind was great in the earth, and that every inclination of the thoughts of their hearts was only evil continually.* [6] *And **the LORD was sorry** that he had made humankind on the earth, and it grieved him to his heart.* [7] *So the LORD said, I will blot out from the earth the human beings I have created people together with animals and creeping things and birds of the air, **for I am sorry** that I have made them."* [Emphasis mine]

The LORD was sorry. So sorry, in fact that God went about UNDOING the creation of humans. God did this, not because

God planned it that way, but because God regretted the outcome of this act. The LORD saw, that is to say, observed that which God had not intended, and went about to reverse the unwanted outcome.

The second occasion is in Genesis 22, with the story of Abraham's willingness to sacrifice Isaac. In 22:7ff, we read,

> *Isaac said to his father Abraham, Father! And he said, Here I am, my son. He said, The fire and the wood are here, but where is the lamb for a burnt offering? ⁸Abraham said, God himself will provide the lamb for a burnt offering, my son. So the two of them walked on together. ⁹When they came to the place that God had shown him, Abraham built an altar there and laid the wood in order. He bound his son Isaac, and laid him on the altar, on top of the wood. ¹⁰Then Abraham reached out his hand and took the knife to kill his son. ¹¹ But the angel of the LORD called to him from heaven, and said, Abraham, Abraham! And he said, Here I am. ¹²He said, Do not lay your hand on the boy or do anything to him; **for now I know** that you fear God, since you have not withheld your son, your only son, from me."* [Emphasis mine]

'…for now I know' Were it not for this reality, this truly not knowing if Abraham were indeed the fit subject for the promised covenant, this whole episode is a sham and a merciless torturing of Abraham. But God did not know, and needed to find out. I hope this isn't too unsettling, as our free will depends upon this.

The third incident is in Exodus, Chapter 32, following the incident of the golden calf, which turns out to be the proverbial last straw, demolishing God's patience with Israel.

Beginning at verse 7,

> *The LORD said to Moses, I have seen this people, how stiff-necked they are. ¹⁰Now let me alone, so that my wrath may burn hot against them and I may consume them; and*

*of you I will make a great nation. 11But Moses implored the
LORD his God, and said, O LORD, why does your wrath
burn hot against your people, whom you brought out of the
land of Egypt with great power and with a mighty hand?
12Why should the Egyptians say, It was with evil intent that
he brought them out to kill them in the mountains, and to
consume them from the face of the earth? Turn from your
fierce wrath; change your mind and do not bring disaster on
your people. 13Remember Abraham, Isaac, and Israel, your
servants, how you swore to them by your own self, saying
to them, I will multiply your descendants like the stars of
heaven, and all this land that I have promised I will give to
your descendants, and they shall inherit it forever. **14And
the LORD changed his mind** about the disaster that he
planned to bring on his people.* [Emphasis mine]

The LORD changed his mind. God was willing to destroy all
of Israel, but for Moses, and begin again with him. Were it not for
Moses' intercession, this story would have had an entirely different
outcome. That's taking this story seriously. I think that this is
taking it and the other examples of God changing God's mind on
their own terms. Think about this: If this were not the case, then
prayer is useless. What Moses did is called intercessory prayer.
Don't Christians believe that prayer works because God can change
outcomes that would have gone otherwise had we not prayed?

I am committed to the notion that what we are living through
in our lives isn't some movie that God is watching with the heavenly
court that never changes no matter how many times it is replayed.
God is indeed watching and wishing to partner with us, and often
does, as we live our lives out together, in an open-ended future.
That's Genesis!

Consistent with what we have seen in God's actions, God's first
experiment to find a suitable helper for the man ended unsuccessfully. It is only after the man turns down every creature presented
to him that God created the woman. Verse 23 is very telling here:

Then the man said, This at last [after all the foregoing effort] *is bone of my bones and flesh of my flesh; this one shall be called Woman, for out of Man this one was taken.*

Among the many details of this story, I find three appropriate for this discussion:

- God's first intention was to limit the initial creation to "the man." The man's loneliness precluded this.
- God's first choice for a companion to the lonely man was not a woman, it was a creature.
- No matter what the man's choice was, it was the man's choice. God did not force the woman on the man; the man told God, this, at last, is the one for him.

God trusted the man to make the appropriate choice. The decision was always the man's. God's role here is facilitator to end the man's loneliness, not the dictator of how to fix the man's loneliness.

There is no way that a doctrine of the exclusivity of heterosexuality can be adduced from this story. If anything, the woman, and sex, are afterthoughts, contingencies required of the changing situation. This is consistent with the texts regarding the experimental nature of God with humanity we've already seen (Genesis 6:5-6; Genesis 22:7-12; Exodus 32:7- 14). Perhaps better put, God is willing to adapt to realities that present themselves owing to the nature of free will and its often unexpected consequences.

From these realities, I ask these questions:

1. Since heterosexuality is a contingency, why can't nonheterosexuals be considered a contingency?

2. Since God allowed "the man" to make his own choice, why is it not consistent for today's nonheterosexual person to make his or her own choice?

3. Since overcoming loneliness is the objective, and since a nonheterosexual's loneliness can't be overcome in a heterosexual

relationship, isn't it proper for a nonheterosexual to find a companion suitable for him or her?

So we need to listen carefully to the stories of creation in Genesis. Since heterosexuality is merely a contingency of creation, what can be adduced from Genesis is heterosexuality, expressed as the procreative ability, is the norm, but certainly not the sole sexuality. Yes, the couple is now told to be fruitful and multiply, and fill the earth and subdue it; but reproductive capability has never been a mandatory criterion for being a full human being who bears the image of God, or for being married.

So, I thank these authors for pointing out to us that one of the great benefits of marriage is that it enables us to overcome our loneliness. Given that God literally moved heaven and earth to accomplish this, shouldn't this same God-like attitude prevail for all of God's children?

Sodom and Gomorrah: Much ado about homosexual nothing—Genesis 19

One of the things that makes biblical interpretation so thorny is the difficulty of moving from one culture to another. If the Bible is read the same way one reads the newspaper, thinking that things then are just like things now, the first mistake is made and a false outcome is guaranteed. This is especially true with the story of Sodom and Gomorrah.

Let's take a step back before we get into the text and see what cultural norms are operating here. The early second millennium BC was a particularly harsh time for desert dwellers. Travel in these days was complicated by bandits, harsh weather and predatory animals. One literally put one's life in jeopardy when traveling. That's why traveling by caravan was so popular. So to alleviate as much misery as possible, a "hospitality ethic" was born.

The hospitality ethic, practiced throughout the Middle East, was to ensure the safe passage of strangers while they traveled. The way it worked is illustrated in the story just preceding this with the arrival of the strangers to Abraham's encampment. Abraham bows down to the strangers, showing greeting, not hostility; Abraham orders a fine dinner prepared for them, and then personally stands watch over them while they ate, as he was now responsible for their safety. This was not done because people in those days were especially nice to each other, or there was an abundance of food to go around. No. It was to ensure that a city or tribe got a good reputation for hospitality so that its citizens, when traveling, would be accorded the same good treatment. If a city had a bad reputation, its travelers would not find a hospitable welcome away from home.

It is in the context of the hospitality ethic that the story of Sodom and Gomorrah unfolds. Aliens come to the home of a resident alien, Lot. This is grounds for grave suspicion. Could they be planning something against us? The citizens demand to have the strangers brought out so they may know (*yadha*) them.

In the Septuagint, the Old Testament translated into Greek about 70 BC, the rabbis translated the Hebrew word *yadha* into a Greek word that can mean "to interrogate" the strangers. The rabbis saw this story as a typical reaction to strangers and the need to know their motives.

It is fairly obvious that the citizens' intention was to rape the strangers. Not "to have sex with them," but to rape them. Lot counters with an offer to allow the men to rape his daughters. (One could digress here and point out that this isn't what any of us would do today. Offering our daughters is not an act of hospitality we would consider appropriate as a host. That's why we can't assume that things then are like things now. Yet, Lot was obliged to make any concession to protect those who came into his home.)

Note: There is nothing consensual in either case, for the strangers or the daughters. Male on male rape was a common aspect of ancient Near Eastern society regarding enemies. Rape was (and still is) an effort to humiliate and control. The usual practice after a war victory was to rape the remaining soldiers into submission as a show of dominance. Ancient Near Eastern museums display artworks depicting this, such as this one on a vase. It depicts a Greek soldier about to rape a defeated and horrified Persian.

This aspect of rape is depicted by the men of Sodom saying, *This fellow* [Lot] *came here as an alien and he would play the judge! Now we will deal worse with you than with them.* They were going to rape Lot, too!

We now know that rape has nothing to do with sex, except that it is done with the genitals. To say that rape is sex is to say that we kiss a drumstick while our lips assist in tearing meat from the bone. Therefore, this is a story of rape, having nothing to do with sex, let alone, homosexual sex.

This story is concerned about abuse of the stranger, not about homosexuals. The sin here has absolutely nothing to do with homosexuals at all.

Here's the witness of the Bible, itself:

• Isaiah 1:10,17

Hear the word of the Lord, you rulers of Sodom! Listen to the teaching of our God, you people of Gomorrah!...Learn to do good; seek justice, rescue the oppressed, defend the orphan, plead for the widow.

- Ezekiel 16:48-50 Regarding Jerusalem
As I live, says the Lord God, your sister Sodom and her daughters have not done as you and your daughters have done. 49 This was the guilt of your sister Sodom: she and her daughters had pride, excess of food, and prosperous ease, but did not aid the poor and needy. 50 They were haughty, and did these abominable things before me; therefore I removed them when I saw it.

- Zephaniah 2:9-10
Therefore, as I live, says the LORD of hosts the God of Israel, Moab shall become like Sodom and the Ammonites like Gomorrah, a land possessed by nettles and salt pits, and a waste forever.
The remnant of my people shall plunder them, and the survivors of my nation shall possess them. 10 This shall be their lot in return for their pride, because they scoffed and boasted against the people of the LORD of hosts.

- Book of Wisdom 19:13-18 (Roman Catholic Bible) Regarding Sodom and Gomorrah
On the sinners, punishment rained down not without violent thunder as early warning; and deservedly they suffered for their crimes, since they evinced such bitter hatred for strangers.

- Church Father, Origen (185-254 C.E.)

Hear this, you who close your homes to guests! Hear this, you who shun the traveler as an enemy! Lot lived among the Sodomites. We do not read of any other good deeds of his:...He escaped the flames, escaped the fire, on account of one thing only. He opened his home to guests. The angels entered the hospitable household; the flames entered those homes closed to guests." (Homilia Vin Genesim)

Leviticus: *When is an abomination not an abomination?*

Here are the two passages in Leviticus that are at the center of the controversy: (Leviticus 18:22) *You shall not lie with a male as with a woman; it is an abomination.* And (Leviticus 20:13) *If a man lies with a male as with a woman, both of them have committed an abomination; they shall be put to death; their blood is upon them.* Quite straightforward, aren't they. After reading this in my seminar, I would close the Bible, and announce that the seminar is over. This is so clear, how could anyone with any credibility believe that God approves of LGBTs after hearing this? Moses wanted them executed; how could this possibly be defended?

One might be excused in believing that this is the last word on the subject if one reads the Bible strictly on a "face value" basis. "It says what it means and means what it says." But that is often a very misleading way to read the Bible, as we shall see.

Just what is meant by a biblical abomination? Here are a couple of other interesting abominations in the stories about Joseph.

Genesis 43:32 *They served him by himself, and them by themselves, because the Egyptians could not eat with the Hebrews, for that is an abomination to the Egyptians.*

Genesis 46:34 *When Pharaoh calls you, and says, 'What is your occupation?' you shall say, 'Your servants have been keepers of livestock from our youth even until now, both we and our ancestors'—in order that you may settle in the land of Goshen, because all shepherds are abhorrent* [toévah] *to the Egyptians.*

Some abominations are clearly culturally derived.

Here are some other notable abominations (all from the Hebrew *toévah*).

- Observing the nakedness of a relative
- Sex during menstruation
- Eating shrimp, lobster, rabbit, pork, etc.
- Wearing of other gender's clothing
- Planting two different crops in the same field
- Wearing clothing of two different fabrics
- Spots on a priest's bald head
- Eating fruit from a tree less than five years old

Abominations, all. So, if you are a woman reading this wearing blue jeans, you are an abomination. If you are anyone wearing a cotton/polyester shirt, you are an abomination. If you are a farmer planting hybrid crops, you are an abomination. If you raise cattle or livestock, all hybrids, you are an abomination. If you had a shrimp cocktail or pulled pork barbeque for dinner last night, you are an abomination.

I think you get the point. However, some miss it entirely, as they know that all these are also biblical abominations which require the trespasser to avoid all such behavior, yet blithely, even cavalierly, think nothing of ignoring these biblical abominations. Yet they insist on holding steadfastly to the one and only one regarding what they think is same-sex lovemaking. (It's not, as discussed below.)

The problem, though, is that this is a package deal. We can't just pick and choose what abominations we will observe and which we will ignore. They all stand or fall together. Some have no problem ignoring the shrimp prohibition or any of the others, except the ONE that bothers them the most. I'll let you decide why this one and only this one is picked as the inviolable one…"because the Bible says so."

But what about the Levitical death penalty?

Yet, this prohibition carries with it capital punishment, as both of them have committed an abomination; they shall be put to death; their blood is upon them. What about it? Shouldn't we place this into a special category? Well, let's see. Here are other Laws that require the death penalty:

- A child cursing one's parents
- A woman's lack of virginity on the wedding night
- Adultery
- Incest
- Working on the Sabbath day

Would those who insist on upholding Leviticus 20:13 insist also on making each of these a capital offense? I think not. So why this ONE and ONLY one?

If we executed every child who cursed its parents, and every person who committed adultery, there would be few adults left to raise the remaining children. (Let alone serve in Congress.) And as loathsome as incest is, we aren't about to begin killing its perpetrators. So let's cut the hypocrisy here and admit that there are no grounds for insisting on keeping the Levitical prohibition in place.

But there is one more piece of work left to do. I introduced the cultural aspect of how abominations are formed with the examples of Joseph in Egypt. In America, I might ask if you had sautéed poodle for dinner last night? That would appall you, wouldn't it. Other cultures might find it appetizing. It is the culture that creates what is approved or not. In Israel, coming into the Canaanite territory, the temptation was always to adopt the habits and mores of their neighbors. *All the prophets railed against this, and Moses stipulated against certain things that would draw the Israelites closer to worshiping Baal. The Lord spoke to Moses, saying: Speak to the people of Israel and say to them: I am the Lord your God. You shall not do as they do in the land of Egypt, where you lived, and you shall not do as they do in the land of Canaan.* (Leviticus 18:3)

One example is male temple prostitution.

(1 Kings 14:24) *...there were also male temple prostitutes in the land. They committed all the abominations of the nations that the Lord drove out before the people of Israel.*

The Levitical prohibition certainly was aimed at forbidding this abomination and may have been the only reason for it, as nowhere in the Mosaic Law is female to female sex banned.

Whom does Paul have in mind in Romans 1?

We need to clear some of the debris out of the way before we can get into the specifics of this most vitriolic of rants by Paul, Romans 1:18-32.

The first observation is that there is no word or combination of words that can be translated "homosexual," or its synonyms, in Greek (or Hebrew, for that matter). Linguists know that without a word there is no concept. So to believe that what we know as homosexuality today existed in the same form 2000 years ago is quite wrong. To use the word homosexual (sodomite, etc.) in an English translation is to put words in apostles' mouths (or in their pens, as it were).

Some translations that use the "Dynamic Equivalent" mode of translation think they found the equivalent in either homosexual or Sodomite, but there is no equivalent extant today. Even the NRSV, a non-Dynamic Equivalent translation, mistranslated the word and has no excuse. So the people who can quote their translation thinking they are quoting the Bible are only misquoting the original.

So, point number one is that whatever it is that Paul is talking about here, it is decidedly not homosexuality as we know it today. The Bible can't condemn that which it knows nothing about.

The Greek word for nature, *physis*, as used by Paul, isn't at all what conservative interpreters want it to mean, that is, equivalent to Natural Law, or the way God made things. Quite to the contrary, as seen in Paul's use of the word in 1 Corinthians 11:14, *Does not nature itself teach you that if a man wears long hair, it is degrading to him...?* One is entitled to ask, in what way does nature teach this? Well, it doesn't. Paul came to his belief about the length of hair by way of his culture's teachings which are received as the way things are (or should be!). My mother was roundly condemned by her mother when she "bobbed" her hair (cut it short) as a young woman in the Roaring Twenties. Grandmother was simply put off because she and her peers were taught that short hair on a woman meant she was "loose." Today, short hair is considered inconsequential. Nature has nothing to do with it.

Troy W. Martin, a medical historian, in an article in the *Journal of Biblical Literature*, tells us how Paul and his contemporaries came to this conclusion about hair. Since the time of Hippocrates to well beyond Paul's day, hair was considered to be a sexual object. The Greek word for hair and testes is the same word. That's why women were to cover their hair, as it was considered erogenous. Hair also had a procreative function. It was thought to be hollow and therefore created a vacuum. This was thought to pull the sperm into the womb. A woman who was not able to conceive had a pungent suppository placed in her vagina and told to return the next day. If the physician could smell the odor in the woman's mouth, she was thought able to conceive; if not, she was considered infertile.

Naturally (if you'll forgive the pun), it worked the same way in the male. Long hair pulled the man's sperm away from the source making procreation more difficult, if not impossible. Therefore, long hair would be deemed unnatural and degrading to a man. Short hair on a woman was, likewise, degrading (why it was often cut off as punishment). Both were rejecting their "natural" roles as procreators.

So, when Paul appeals to "nature," he is merely reflecting the notions of his culture and not relaying truth fallen from heaven. His information is only as good as his culture can make it. Christians are under no obligation to follow it.

The most despicable people in the world

We can "cut to the chase" very quickly by beginning at the end. To see where Paul is headed is to see what concerns him. And it should concern us, too.

Whoever it is that Paul is castigating here surely are among humanity's most despicable people. Here's how the NRSV puts it:

They were filled with every kind of wickedness, evil, covetousness, malice. Full of envy, murder, strife, deceit, craftiness, they are gossips, slanderers, God-haters, insolent, haughty, boastful, inventors of evil, rebellious toward parents, foolish, faithless, heartless, ruthless. They know God's decree, that those who practice such things deserve to die— yet they not only do them but even applaud others who practice them.

No one of wholesome spirit would want to be associated with such as these. This is character shaped by idolatry; that is, shaped by other than God.

We begin here because I want you to consider something in your own experience. Do you know any Christian LGBTs who fit this description? Certainly not. They fit, instead, another of Paul's lists of characteristics, the fruit of the Spirit: love, joy, peace, patience, kindness, generosity, faithfulness. If this isn't your experience, you don't know enough gay Christians! Therefore, I can say with assurance that whomever Paul has in mind, it isn't gay Christians!

It must also be said that this does not fit even the vast majority of LGTB people at all. The prejudicial depiction of the stereotypical gay is a product of projecting a minority of gays as typical of the whole. Even in a pride parade, the exhibitionists are in the minority.

I know hundreds of LGBT Christians, many of whom make my witness look puny. I also know gays who have been driven from our churches by behavior more typical of the strife, deceit, craftiness, gossip, slanderer, insolent, haughty, boastful behavior that Paul decries, than that of the Spirit.

Have we misread the Bible?

The history of interpreting Romans 1 has taken a turn in recent scholarship. One of the most important insights came from asking a simple question: If what we know as sexual orientation (that is, heterosexuality, homosexuality and the like) is a product of modern psychological study, and are foreign concepts in biblical days, have we misread the Bible? Another way of putting the question is, Have we assumed that Paul has these modern categories in mind in Romans 1? If we do not, and I believe we shouldn't or we are invoking anachronisms, then a whole new outcome is revealed, one that can no longer support the view that Paul is denouncing gays and lesbians. How can this be?

Not only did Paul not work with the unknown (to his age) categories of sexual orientation, he did not even think in terms of homosexual behavior, either. Sex for him and his Greco-Roman contemporaries was ethical or unethical, appropriate or inappropriate. Worst of all was sex that was driven by passion.

A revealing notion from a Greek philosopher, Dio Chrysostom, (a contemporary of Paul) is that he assumed that the same lust that drove a man to seek intercourse with women would lead the same man to intercourse with men. He would think this because sexual orientation was not a category known to him; passion drove sexual desire. Lust, or passion, was considered the most harmful of the influences on one's life. The ideal man (sic) is the one who is virtually passionless, who is always in full control of his emotions.

This is easily seen in the way that Luke (the author of this Gospel is a classically trained Greek) eliminates the emotions from Mark's depictions of Jesus. Here are just a couple of examples.

Mark 4:20 *And these are the ones sown on the good soil; they hear the word and accept it and bear fruit, thirty and sixty and a hundredfold.*

Luke adds the description of the ideal person. Luke 8:15 *But as for that in the good soil, these are the ones who, when they hear the word, hold it fast in an honest and good heart, and bear fruit with patient endurance.*

Mark 3:5 *He looked around at them with anger; he was grieved at their hardness of heart and said to the man, "Stretch out your hand."* Luke omits the emotions altogether. Luke 6:10 *After looking around at all of them, he said to him, "Stretch out your hand."* Take out your concordance and see for yourself how many times Luke omits Mark's emotions from Jesus. His Jesus is the Hellenistic perfect man, virtually devoid of emotion.

With this in mind let's take a closer look at 1:26-27 (NRSV)

So Paul wrote: *For this reason God gave them up to degrading passions. Their women exchanged natural intercourse for unnatural, and in the same way also the men, giving up natural intercourse with women, were consumed with passion for one another. Men committed shameless acts with men and received in their own persons the due penalty for their error.*

If we don't immediately assume lesbianism at work here in *Their women exchanged natural intercourse for unnatural*, it isn't necessary to import it. It is open to a variety of meanings. And the expression in the same way also the men means that passion invaded their bodies just like it invaded the women's bodies. So the due penalty for their error was indeed received in their own persons, that is, in their own bodies, that despicable source of all evil, passion.

When we delve deeply into the prevailing context of the biblical era, we discover an almost impenetrable distance. So different, in fact, that we end up comparing apples with oranges, or in this case, equating modern sexual orientation with a Stoic distaste of emotion and think they are the same thing. They are not. The notion that two people of the same sex could love each other and be as committed to one another as any heterosexual couple was as foreign to him as this idolatry/passion related explanation is to us. Surely only stubbornness can explain why people continue to believe our present day LGBTs fit this description. For the source of their orientations, we must look elsewhere. Romans 1 needs to be removed from the index of charges against them. Yes, idolatry has its casualties; let's not add LGBTs to that list.

Is it possible for a gay's sexual orientation to be changed from gay to straight?—*1 Corinthians 6:9-11*

Herman Goebbels was right: tell a lie often enough and soon it will be thought to be the truth. Such a lie has been circulating for a few decades now, but is finally being held up to the light of truth, scientific truth to be exact. It is the lie that gays can be made straight through proper counseling and prayer. It's been stylized as

"Pray away the gay," in many conservative Christian churches and movements.

So, what drives the conservative Christian movement to accept this lie at face value? Very simply, it's all about one short paragraph in the Bible, 1 Corinthians 6:9-11.

*Do you not know that wrongdoers will not inherit the kingdom of God? Do not be deceived! Fornicators, idolaters, adulterers, male prostitutes, **sodomites**, thieves, the greedy, drunkards, revilers, rob-bers—none of these will inherit the kingdom of God. And **this is what some of you used to be**. But you were washed, you were sanctified, you were justified in the name of the Lord Jesus Christ and in the Spirit of our God.* [Emphasis mine]

This verse straightforwardly states that some in the con-gregation were once sodomites, but are no longer. Sodomites, erroneously, are understood to be today's homosexuals. Many gay Christians took this verse to heart and subjected themselves to every conceivable treatment to rid themselves of this condition because they believed what they read. (Mel White estimates he paid nearly $500,000 in efforts to change his orientation, including shock treatments.) However, this verse does not actually say anything of the kind. The translation, sodomites, was not coined until 1000 years after the Bible was written, so its use here is anachronistic. Therefore, a more suitable translation is required, and one is at hand: users of temple prostitutes. Male prostitutes were temple prostitutes in Corinth and they had customers/users. These are the people under consideration in this paragraph, and no wonder Paul could claim that they were washed, they were sanctified, they were justified in the name of the Lord Jesus Christ....But to expect the same for nonheterosexuals isn't warranted or even possible, and NOT under consideration in this paragraph.

Here's a sampling of what experts in their fields have to say about the impossibility of changing sexual orientation and the harm it causes:

American Academy of Pediatrics (1993)

Therapy directed specifically at changing sexual orientation is contraindicated, since it can provoke guilt and anxiety while having little or no potential for achieving changes in orientation. American Medical Association (2003)

Our AMA opposes the use of 'reparative' or 'conversion' therapy that is based on the assumption that homosexuality per se is a mental disorder or based upon the a priori assumption that the patient should change his/her homosexual orientation. American Psychoanalytic Association (2000)

Psychoanalytic technique does not encompass purposeful efforts to 'convert' or 'repair' an individual's sexual orientation. Such directed efforts are against fundamental principles of psychoanalytic treatment and often result in substantial psychological pain by reinforcing damaging internalized homophobic attitudes.

American Psychiatric Association (1998)

The American Psychiatric Association opposes any psychiatric treatment, such as reparative or conversion therapy, which is based upon the assumption that homosexuality per se is a mental disorder or based upon the priori assumption that a patient should change his/her sexual homosexual orientation. The APA removed homosexuality from its list of disorders in 1973.

American Psychological Association (1997)

No scientific evidence exists to support the effectiveness of any of the conversion therapies that try to change sexual orientation. The association removed homosexuality from its list of disorders in 1975.

National Association of Social Workers (2000)

People seek mental health services for many reasons. Accordingly, it is fair to assert that lesbians and gay men seek therapy for the same reasons that heterosexual people do. However, the increase in media campaigns, often coupled with coercive messages from family and community members, has created an environment in which lesbians and gay men often are pressured to seek reparative or conversion therapies, which cannot and will not change sexual orientation.... Specifically, transformational ministries are fueled by stigmatization of lesbians and gay men, which in turn produces the social climate that pressures some people to seek change in sexual orientation. No data demonstrate that reparative or conversion therapies are effective, and in fact they may be harmful.

Gays can't change their orientation any more than straights can. Since God made each of us in our own special way, why would we want to?

Here's a snippet of a video from a documentary I was involved with that looks at these passages.

I am commenting on Leviticus about two minutes into the clip. http://www.youtube.com/watch?feature=player_detail-page&v=JDKL-f9Iwds

THE ANTI-GAY INDUSTRY

Not everyone in America is of the same mind on the subject of homosexuality, as I am sure you know. This is not to say that reasonable minds can disagree and we can leave it at that. You see, the opposition, for the most part, is unreasonable to the point of obstinacy. Why? They are most often driven by ideology, not the search for reliable facts or even interested at all in you or your children's well-being. A recent apology from a long-time lobbyist for the largest anti-gay ministry in the world, Randy Thomas, underscores this. Here is part of what he admitted to:

> I participated in the hurtful echo chamber of con-demnation. I gave lip service to the gay community, but really did not exemplify compassion for them. I placed the battle over policy [ideology] above my concern for real people. I sometimes valued the shoulder pats I was given by religious leaders more than Jesus' com-mandment to love and serve. That was wrong and I'm disappointed in myself. Please forgive me. https://www.truthwinsout.org/news/2013/07/36367/

Here's how it works. For these religious, they are convinced that the Bible condemns LGBTs and nothing, NOTHING can persuade them to the contrary. They are often the same people who

believe that AIDS is God's judgment on homosexuals, notwith-
standing the reality that over 99% of its victims are heterosexual.
(It's a strange god indeed who would destroy millions of people
to get at a mere handful.) They have a pseudoscience on their side
called Reparative Therapy, discussed above, that has been thorough-
ly repudiated by mainstream authorities. Exodus International, the
original and largest of the ex-gay movements, for decades insisting
that gays can be made straight, recently called it quits because, as
their president put it, there is simply no evidence that gays can
change.

These anti-gay advocates include James Dobson from Focus on
the Family, the National Organization for Marriage, the American
Family Association, NARTH, and the Family Research Council,
among others. If you take the time to look over their websites
you will discover that they all basically share the same information which is drawn from the same pool of discredited studies and
movements

You can read all about these implacable people at http://www.
exgaywatch.com, http://www.truthwinsout.org, and http://www.
boxturtlebulletin.com/.

For those who are not coming at this from a religious perspective, and there are precious few, the only explanation is latent
homosexuality (or even overt) that creates a revolting response to
that which they hate in themselves. There are hundreds of known
cases that support this conclusion.

George Rekers, a man who helped start one of the most
powerful anti-gay lobbying groups in the US published the tract,
"Growing Up Straight: What Families Should Know About Homosexuality", was caught red-handed with a male prostitute he secured
from http:/www.rentboy.com. This site has since been seized by the
Department of Homeland Security.

Alabama Attorney General Troy King, well-known for his vo-
cal opposition to gay rights, King was caught by his wife while
having sex with the homecoming king from Troy University.

Glenn Murphy Jr., erstwhile head of the Young Republicans and formerly a leading Republican in Indiana, was known for promoting "family values" and using anti-gay rhetoric. He was caught for the second time we know of, performing fellatio on another Young Republican while that man slept, without that man's consent. He is now a convicted felon and a registered sex offender.

We could go on and on with this, but enough is enough. There is just one more important piece of information to impart. As reported in an American Psychological Association press release in August 1996 entitled, "New Study Links Homophobia with Homosexual Arousal," one source of homophobia is latent homosexuality.

The people funding and/or heading up the organizations that promote anti-gay positions do not have you or your child's best interest at heart. They are merely defending a position that they deem more important than the well-being of anyone. They are committed to the proposition that gayness is an evil that needs to be stamped out, regardless of how it affects lives and the dubious means used to support their cause. I simply don't want you to be taken in. I also don't want you to just take my word for it. Do your own research and see where it takes you. After twenty years of doing so myself, this is the conclusion I've reached. Remember, your child is perfectly fine. Those who want you to believe otherwise have nothing to support their cause and ignore the mountain of evidence to the contrary.

This time I don't have a video for you, but I have a great blogsite. http://holybulliesandheadlessmonsters.blogspot.com/ As the blogger says, "Lies in the name of God are still lies." I highly recommend checking this blog out.

A GREAT RESOURCE FOR ADDITIONAL HELP AND UNDERSTANDING

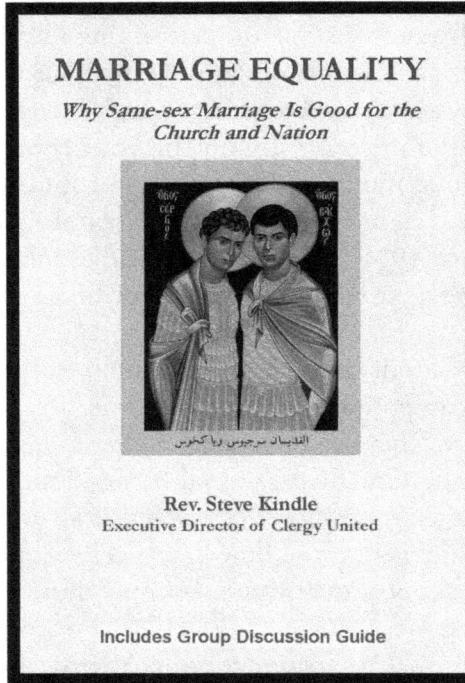

MARRIAGE EQUALITY
Why Same-sex Marriage Is Good for the Church and Nation

Rev. Steve Kindle
Executive Director of Clergy United

Includes Group Discussion Guide

(If I say so myself)

The section on "What Does the Bible Say" is taken from part of a chapter in my new book, *Marriage Equality: Why it's good for the church and nation.* It covers much more ground than the title focus, as I go into depth about the most pressing issues facing the gay community, the lies, misrepresentations, and misunderstandings that support gay opposition, and a comprehensive look at what makes up gay America. If you want to go deeper into the subject, I invite you to check it out on Energion Publications here:

Again, if you wish to contact me, I can be reached at mailto:info@clergyunited.org, and will do what I can to assist you. My website, http://www.clergyunited.org, has more helpful material.

ALSO BY REV. STEVE KINDLE

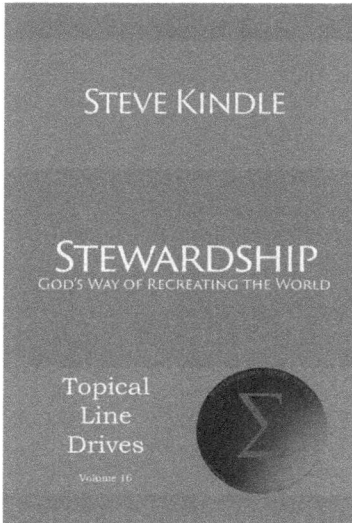

STEVE KINDLE

STEWARDSHIP
GOD'S WAY OF RECREATING THE WORLD

Topical
Line
Drives

Volume 16

Σ

Reconnect with the biblical notion of **stewardship** as a way of life.

Why do well-meaning, intelligent people disagree about the Bible?

STEVE KINDLE

I'M RIGHT
AND
YOU'RE WRONG
WHY WE DISAGREE ABOUT THE BIBLE
AND
WHAT TO DO ABOUT IT

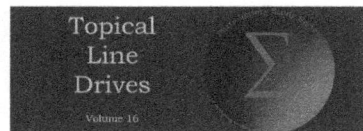

Topical
Line
Drives

Volume 16

Σ